WERE YOU THERE?

WERE YOU THERE?

Four meditations on the theme
of Easter

By

ALLEN BIRTWHISTLE
M.A., B.Sc.

LONDON : : THE EPWORTH PRESS

PUBLISHED BY

THE EPWORTH PRESS

(FRANK H. CUMBERS)

25-35 CITY ROAD, LONDON, E.C.1

*

New York : Toronto
Melbourne : Capetown

*

*Printed in England by Page & Thomas Ltd.
Sheraton Street, London, W.1, and at Chesham*

CONTENTS

ACKNOWLEDGEMENTS

I am grateful to the United Society for Christian Literature for permission to use two poems from *The Infinite Christ* by Chandran Devanesen; to H. R. Allenson Ltd. for the prayer by James Martineau taken from *Great Souls at Prayer*; to the Lutterworth Press, for permission to quote from *The Planting of Christianity in Africa*, Vol. I, by C. P. Groves; and to the International Missionary Council for allowing me to quote from *The World Mission of the Church* (findings of the Tambaram Conference). The Rev. Donald S. Ching has kindly given permission for me to include his hitherto unpublished poem 'Let the boy play here', and I am indebted to the Rev. Ernest Porter for drawing my attention to the cruciform page before St. Matthew in the *Lindisfarne Gospels*.

INTRODUCTION

THE first part of this book comprises talks given at the beginning of each day during the Watford Circuit Young People's Easter Conference held at Chorley Wood College in 1949. The Study Notes on the Cross which form the second part were used in the discussion groups at that conference.

In these days of bewilderment caused by mistrust between the nations, by the impact of secularism on faith and conduct, and the difficulty which a so-called scientific age experiences in accepting Christian beliefs, many young people seek to escape from confusion by finding refuge in the cult of Service. But service offers no escape from frustration unless there be purpose in it—and that demands an awareness of the purpose of life. The Communist is ready with his explanation of the meaning of every event in its widest, infinite, setting, and we do well to remind ourselves that the Christian is a person aware of God's Design in His Universe. This design not only covers the sweep of history but also takes up the details of our lives ; and it comes to a focus in the Cross. That is where this book starts : with the Purpose of God as shown in the Cross ; it ends with our service as seen in the light of the Cross.

The chapters begin with a question and arrive at an affirmation. In each there is a brief account of some great English Christian : Gilbert, Ridley, Bede, and Tyndale ; and each concludes with part of the Covenant Service, the greatest contribution of Methodism to the liturgy of the World Church.

The Study Notes on the Cross at the end of this volume began as a brief outline for use by groups of Cambridge University students in preparation for a campaign. They were enlarged and have been used by the Young Men's League, and form the first of a series of pamphlets designed to help groups to discover God's Purpose for them as it is revealed in the Bible, in terms of the World Church, and in the light of contemporary events.

PART ONE

GOOD FRIDAY

Were You There?

THE scientific staff of the Admiralty Research Station at Perranporth have analysed the swell off the Cornish coast and have been able to identify the distant storm centres from which the waves began.[1] By a neat calculation depending on the fact that a storm generates waves of different periods and that different waves travel at different speeds, they have traced a twelve-inch movement at Perranporth a distance of nearly seven thousand miles back to a region of the South Atlantic between Cape Horn and the Falkland Islands.

We do not stand in any such relation to the storm which broke in Jerusalem two thousand years ago. We are not receiving-stations detecting the last faint ripples of a dying controversy. We are in the thick of it still, and there is only one answer to the haunting question of the Negro spiritual :

> Were you there when they crucified my Lord?
> Were you there when they crucified my Lord?
> O, sometimes, it causes me to tremble,
> Were you there when they crucified my Lord?

If we have ever, by look or by word or by silence, joined in the condemnation of an innocent person, we are standing in the Sanhedrin there with Caiaphas. If we have ever been weak and allowed things to go through

[1] See *Science News*, No. 10 (Penguin Books).

which we knew we ought to have challenged, because in challenging them we should have seemed eccentric or might have brought trouble upon ourselves, we are sitting on the judgement bench with Pilate. If I have ever betrayed my Lord even at the moment when I was at His table, I am dipping in the dish there with Judas. If I have denied Him through lack of courage, I am there with Peter warming myself at the fire.

> My mind is for ever splintered
> on the anvil of Time
> and my spirit wanders restlessly
> through the caverns of Eternity.
> You ask me why?
> I was an ordinary legionary in Jerusalem
> nigh two thousand years ago.
> One chill, windy morning
> we nailed a Man to a cross.
> (It was a routine job.)
> He died rather soon.
> I remember throwing down the dice
> (we were gambling for His clothes),
> and, picking up my spear, a trusty weapon
> that had seen me through many a skirmish
> in Gaul and Libya,
> I thrust it into His side
> to make certain before telling the centurion.
> I saw water and blood trickle down the haft
> gripped in my hands.
> I saw more—though, by the bird of Jupiter,
> I wish I hadn't.
> Looking into His deathless eyes
> I saw His heart was broken
> for me.[1]

Fragment from Golgotha, from *The Infinite Christ* by Chandran Devanesen.

Were you there ? Yes, we were there—or, if you prefer it, we *are* there—right in the storm centre. But do not let us flatter ourselves that our sin is the dominant force. It is not the design of Caiaphas or the order of Pilate that rules in the affairs of men, but the Word and Purpose of God ; it is the witness and constancy of God's love that bring hope and renewal into our lives, not the treachery of Judas or the denial of Peter. The dominant force in the Crucifixion was God's Purpose, God's Love, His Plan for us. That is what we mean when we say that on that day the Judge was neither Herod nor Pilate, but Jesus.

In the middle of the eighteenth century Francis Gilbert was living in England. He was the son of a wealthy West Indian Colonist and could afford the gay life of a beau of that period. Francis was converted by the preaching of the Wesleys and he wrote to his brother Nathaniel in the West Indies, sending him some Methodist pamphlets. Nathaniel Gilbert was a very different person from his wandering brother, and he was not likely to waste his substance in riotous living—the story has some affinities with that of the Prodigal Son. He was a lawyer by profession, the owner of two sugar estates in Antigua, and a man of piety and high character. To him the enthusiasm of the Methodists was repulsive, and the pamphlets were put away unread.

Later he fell ill, and when he was recovering he sent Mary, his five-year old daughter, for a book. By mistake she returned with one of the forgotten pamphlets : it was John Wesley's *An Earnest Appeal to Men of Reason and Religion*. Perhaps Nathaniel had a sense of humour after all, at any rate he had plenty of time on his hands and he read the pamphlet through. It impressed him so greatly that he came to London two years later specially to hear John Wesley preach. On 17th February 1758, in a drawing-room meeting at Wandsworth, Wesley conducted a service and Nathaniel Gilbert was there with three of his slaves. The slaves were converted and Nathaniel entered into a new religious experience. When he returned to Antigua he began preaching at his own house, and one Sunday evening he had the bell rung to call his slaves together. That service, held in the largest room of his estate house and packed to the door with slaves, was the first Methodist service held for heathen people ; it was the origin of West Indian Methodism and the start of the Methodist Missionary Society.

There the Cross was preached to people who were enslaved. It *always* is *!* As Wesley himself wrote :

> Long my imprisoned spirit lay,
> Fast bound in sin and nature's night.

The picture is that of a man who has lost his freedom ; a prisoner in a dungeon deep below the ground longing for light and liberty which he can't achieve by his own efforts. The sinner is a man in bondage to the wrong master from whom he can never hope to buy the rights and privileges of those who are free.

AN ACT OF DEVOTION

A hymn by Charles Wesley which combines the two threads of our thought : Were you there ? and the Cross setting us free from the chains of sin is No. 200 in the *Methodist Hymn-book* :

O Jesus, my hope,
For me offered up,
Who with clamour pursued Thee to Calvary's top,
The blood Thou hast shed,
For me let it plead,
And declare Thou hast died in Thy murderer's stead.

Come then from above,
Its hardness remove,
And vanquish my heart with the sense of Thy love ;
Thy love on the tree
Display unto me,
And the servant of sin in a moment is free.

Neither passion nor pride
Thy Cross can abide,
But melt in the fountain that streams from Thy side :
Let Thy life-giving blood
Remove all my load,
And purge my foul conscience, and bring me to God.

Now, now let me know
Its virtue below,
Let it wash me, and I shall be whiter than snow ;
Let it hallow my heart,
And throughly convert,
And make me, O Lord, in the world as Thou art.

Each moment applied
My weakness to hide,
Thy blood be upon me, and always abide :
My Advocate prove
With the Father above,
And speak me at last to the throne of Thy love.   Amen.

The Reading

When Pilate saw that he prevailed nothing, but rather

that a tumult was arising, he took water, and washed his hands before the multitude, saying, I am innocent of the blood of this righteous man : see ye to it. And all the people answered and said, His blood be on us, and on our children. Then released he unto them Barabbas : but Jesus he scourged and delivered to be crucified. Then the soldiers of the governor took Jesus into the place, and gathered unto him the whole band. And they stripped him, and put on him a scarlet robe. And they plaited a crown of thorns and put it upon his head, and a reed in his right hand ; and they kneeled down before him, and mocked him, saying, Hail, King of the Jews ! And they spat upon him, and took the reed and smote him on the head. And when they had mocked him, they took off from him the robe, and put on him his garments, and led him away to crucify him. And as they came out, they found a man of Cyrene, Simon by name : him they compelled to go with them, that he might bear his cross. And when they were come unto a place called Golgotha, that is to say, The place of a skull, they gave him wine to drink mingled with gall : and when he had tasted it, he would not drink. And when they had crucified him, they parted his garments among them, casting lots : And they sat and watched him there. And they set up over his head his accusation written, THIS IS JESUS THE KING OF THE JEWS. Then are there crucified with him two robbers, one on the right hand, and one on the left. And they that passed by railed on him, wagging their heads, and saying, Thou that destroyest the temple, and buildest it in three days, save thyself : if thou art the Son of God, come down from the cross. In like manner also the chief priests mocking him, with the scribes and elders, said, He saved others ; himself he cannot save (Matthew 27^{24-42a}).

The Collect for Good Friday

Almighty God, we beseech Thee graciously to behold this Thy family, for which our Lord Jesus Christ was contented to be betrayed, and given up into the hands of wicked men, and to suffer death upon the cross, who now liveth and reigneth with Thee and the Holy Ghost, ever one God, world without end. Amen.

THE PURPOSE OF THE CROSS

The *Lindisfarne Gospels* are now one of the treasures of the British Museum. They were written out by hand twelve hundred years ago during the time of political chaos which followed the collapse of the Roman Provincial system of government. At that time convents provided shelter for artists who wanted to go on quietly with their work. The style of the illuminations in the *Lindisfarne Gospels* is Celtic, showing a strong Irish influence that came into Northumbria from Iona.

One of the loveliest designs in the book is the page before St. Matthew. It began with a Celtic symbol of the rise and development of man and the figures are springing curves representing the phoenix. Imposed upon it is the design of the Cross. Though the Cross is quite alien in shape and meaning to the original pattern the artist has brought the two together and fused them into new and graceful rhythms. That is what God did with the Cross. In its jagged ugliness the Cross is our pattern superimposed on God's Design. But God has taken it up into His Purpose. And the Purpose? God's Design is to restore man to that pattern of abundant life which was the first will of God for us.

It is a work of salvage, of taking useless, perished

15

2

valueless things and making out of them something that can serve a useful end. We became familiar with the process during the war when rusty metal and dirty scraps of paper, bones and rags and all the rubbish of the dustbin were collected and transformed by the alchemy of modern science into gleaming bright newly-fashioned things with a purpose to serve. A recent notice about a jumble sale appealed to the ladies to give 'articles thought to be of no further use.' Many people smiled at the expression, probably thinking of the pen wipers and egg-cosies that they had bought at previous sales which could now be worked off in the good cause. But we are in that category ourselves until the Cross has done its work for us; until it has transformed us from sinners to sinners saved by grace; until our broken lives have been salvaged by the love of God.

The work of salvaging is not completed by applying a coat of varnish to the surface of the discarded object. Nothing as superficial as that will satisfy the need. One of the surest ways of starting an argument in East Anglia is to begin talking about fen drainage, but one point in the debate is admitted by everyone, and that is that fen drainage is a problem of *depth*. Below the black spongy soil of the fens is a layer of clay through which the water cannot pass. In some places the clay is only a few feet down beneath the surface, at other places it lies at a depth of twenty or thirty feet. When the floods come the water doesn't just sit on the top of the soil but it penetrates down to the clay so that mile after mile of the black earth is drowned to the roots. A few bucketsful pumped off the top make no difference to a mess like that: you have to shift the water that is thirty feet deep as well. The redemption of man in the Purpose of God goes down to the foundations of personality : below the crust we show to everyone else and down to the hidden sources of action.

But redemption not only goes *deep*, down into our present personality, it goes *back*, right into the past to the sins we have tried to forget. The sins of last year are not written off *until God has written them off*. This was the problem that agitated the mind of John Donne in his poem *To Christ* :

> Wilt thou forgive that sinn, where I begunn,
>> Which is my sinn, though it were done before ?
> Wilt thou forgive those sinns through which I runn
>> And doe run still, though still I doe deplore ?
>>> When thou has done, thou hast not done,
>>>> For I have more.
>
> Wilt thou forgive that sinn, by which I'have wonne
>> Others to sinn, and made my sinn their dore ?
> Wilt thou forgive that sinn which I did shunne
>> A yeare or twoe, but wallowed in a score ?
>>> When thou hast done, thou hast not done,
>>>> For I have more.
>
> I have a sinn of feare that when I have spunn
>> My last thred, I shall perish on the shore ;
> Sweare by thy self that at my Death, thy Sonne
>> Shall shine as he shines nowe, & heretofore ;
>>> And having done that, thou hast done,
>>>> I feare noe more.

The purpose of the Cross is what John Donne saw it needed to be, the saving of man to the uttermost—past, present, and future ; and when we see it in action the wonder is what God is able to do with such poor material as ourselves. In Guernsey is the beautiful little Church of Les Vauxbelets. It is quite tiny and it is surrounded by lovely little grottos and gardens which are all the work of a recluse. All this beauty has been created out of broken things! Clinker from the fires of the tomato sheds, which seem to be everywhere in the island, is the main substance of the walls. They have been smoothed over, and covered everywhere—inside and outside the Church, inside the grottos and round the gardens—by designs made up of broken pottery. Over long years and with infinite patience the pattern has taken shape. People all over the world have heard about it and when they have dropped a piece of lovely china, or a kitchen cup, after the first explosion of annoyance they have remembered Father Pierre and parcelled up the pieces and posted them to him. Day after day the parcels have arrived and sometimes he has waited years for the right piece, a portion of the work meanwhile standing unfinished, a bare gap in the general design. So God in His patience waits for us and when we come to Him He has a place awaiting us, a place which no one else can fill.

The Purpose of the Cross is the salvation of man, the remaking of broken human lives, and by what it has done for men it shows the fertility of sacrifice. Grains of wheat which had been sheltered in an earthenware vessel for thousands of years in one of the tombs of Egypt would not grow when they were planted, but the wheat which has gone on struggling and dying is still alive in the outer world ; in fact it is said that the whole Canadian wheat harvest is descended from a single ear of corn. So we come from our thinking about the Cross to one of the great statements of Jesus :

EXCEPT A GRAIN OF WHEAT FALL INTO THE EARTH AND DIE, IT ABIDETH BY ITSELF ALONE; BUT IF IT DIE, IT BEARETH MUCH FRUIT (JOHN 12[24]).

A hymn of Johann Heermann, translated by Robert
Bridges, takes up the ideas of our joining in the crucifixion,
our release from slavery and our salvation through the
Cross (*M.H.B.*, No. 177) :

Ah, holy Jesu, how hast Thou offended,
That man to judge Thee hath in hate pretended ?
By foes derided, by Thine own rejected,
   O most afflicted.

Who was the guilty ? Who brought this upon Thee ?
Alas, my treason, Jesu, hath undone Thee ;
'Twas I, Lord Jesu, I it was denied Thee :
   I crucified Thee.

Lo, the good Shepherd for the sheep is offered ;
The slave hath sinned, and the Son hath suffered ;
For man's atonement, while he nothing heedeth,
   God intercedeth.

For me, kind Jesu, was Thy incarnation,
Thy mortal sorrow, and Thy life's oblation ;
Thy death of anguish and Thy bitter passion,
   For my salvation.

Therefore, kind Jesu, since I cannot pay Thee,
I do adore Thee, and will ever pray Thee,
Think on Thy pity and Thy love unswerving,
   Not my deserving. Amen.

An Act of Adoration (from the Covenant Service) :

MINISTER :
 Let us adore the Father, the God of love who created
  us ;
 Who every moment preserves and sustains us ;
 Who has loved us with an everlasting love, and given
  us the light of the knowledge of His glory in the face
  of Jesus Christ.

PEOPLE :

> We praise Thee, O God, we acknowledge Thee to be the Lord.

MINISTER :

> Let us glory in the grace of our Lord Jesus Christ ;
> Who, though He was rich, yet for our sakes became poor ;
> Who went about doing good and preaching the Gospel of the Kingdom ;
> Who was tempted in all points like as we are, yet without sin ;
> Who became obedient unto death, even the death of the Cross ;
> Who was dead, and liveth for evermore ;
> Who opened the Kingdom of Heaven to all believers ;
> Who sitteth at the right hand of God in the glory of the Father.

PEOPLE :

> Thou art the King of Glory, O Christ.

MINISTER :

> Let us rejoice in the fellowship of the Holy Spirit, the Lord and Giver of life, by whom we are born into the family of God, and made members of the Body of Christ ;
> Whose witness confirm us ;
> Whose wisdom teaches us ;
> Whose power enables us ;
> Who waits to do for us exceeding abundantly above all that we ask or think.

PEOPLE :

> All praise to Thee, O Holy Spirit.

A prayer:

MINISTER :   Lamb of God, whose dying love
           We now recall to mind,
        Send the answer from above,
           And let us mercy find ;
        Think on us, who think on Thee ;
    And every struggling soul release ;

PEOPLE :   O remember Calvary,
        And bid us go in peace !

MINISTER :   By Thine agonizing pain
        And sweat of blood, we pray,
    By Thy dying love to man,
        Take all our sins away :
    Burst our bonds, and set us free ;
  From all iniquity release ;

PEOPLE :   O remember Calvary,
        And bid us go in peace '

MINISTER :   Let Thy blood, by faith applied,
        The sinner's pardon seal ;
    Speak us freely justified,
        And all our sickness heal ;
    By Thy passion on the tree,
  Let all our griefs and troubles cease ;

PEOPLE :   O remember Calvary,
        And bid us go in peace ! Amen.

SATURDAY

Why Are You Here?

A PLAY called *The Cup*[1] is based on the story of the Last Supper and it takes up a suggestion made by scholars as to the inscription which may have appeared round the rim of the chalice which Jesus used. One cup, which is thought to be first-century Sidonian work, has a drinking-legend in Greek letters which runs : WHAT ARE YOU HERE FOR ? BE MERRY. In the light of discoveries about similar writings on ancient drinking-vessels it seems likely that the full inscription which was often used was : COMRADE, WHAT ARE YOU HERE FOR ? BE MERRY.

If these sentences were written on the cup from which the disciples drank at that first communion service, they would have read very strangely on the following day. Without the last two words of encouragement to conviviality, there is a haunting solemnity about the question which would not have been discordant with the mood of bewilderment in which these scattered men found themselves. Why, indeed, were they there ?—in hiding, without hope or courage to face the day. Like Elijah after he had run from the threat of Queen Jezebel, they might well have heard the word of the Lord : ' What doest thou here ? '

The Reading

And Ahab told Jezebel all that Elijah had done, and withal how he had slain all the prophets with the sword.

[1] By Miss Doris M. Gill (published by The Methodist Youth Department).

Then Jezebel sent a messenger unto Elijah, saying, So let the gods do to me, and more also, if I make not thy life as the life of one of them by tomorrow about this time. And when he saw that, he arose, and went for his life, and came to Beer-sheba, which belongeth to Judah, and left his servant there. But he himself went a day's journey into the wilderness, and came and sat down under a juniper tree : and he requested for himself that he might die ; and said, It is enough ; now, O Lord, take away my life ; for I am not better than my fathers. And he lay down and slept under a juniper tree ; and, behold, an angel touched him, and said unto him, Arise and eat. And he looked, and, behold, there was at his head a cake baken on the coals, and a cruse of water. And he did eat and drink, and laid him down again. And the angel of the Lord came again the second time, and touched him, and said, Arise and eat ; because the journey is too great for thee. And he arose, and did eat and drink, and went in the strength of that meat forty days and forty nights unto Horeb the mount of God. And he came thither unto a cave, and lodged there : and, behold, the word of the Lord came to him, and he said unto him, What doest thou here, Elijah ? And he said, I have been very jealous for the Lord, the God of hosts ; for the children of Israel have forsaken thy covenant, thrown down thine altars, and slain thy prophets with the sword : and I, even I only, am left ; and they seek my life, to take it away. And he said, Go forth, and stand upon the mount before the Lord. And, behold, the Lord passed by, and a great and strong wind rent the mountains, and brake in pieces the rocks before the Lord ; but the Lord was not in the wind : and after the wind an earthquake ; but the Lord was not in the earthquake : and after the earthquake a fire ; but the Lord was not in the fire : and after the fire a still small voice. And it was so, when Elijah heard it, that he wrapped his face in his mantle, and went out, and stood in the entering in of the cave. And, behold, there came a voice unto him, and said, What doest thou here, Elijah ? (1 Kings 19$^{1-13}$).

What doest thou here ? No, not just what are you doing at this moment, but what are you doing with your life ? The moody sense of frustration which possesses those of us who do not know very clearly what we are doing with our lives, the feeling of being pushed about by forces we cannot control which is the result of having no direction to our inner life, the aimlessness of not being sure why we are here which is so common among young people today, is well expressed in a poem called *Sea-side Confession*, by the Indian, Chandran Devanesen :

> Lord,
>> When I think I am strong
>> like some rock cape with rugged, defiant walls,
>> the pitiless winds tear layers from me,
>> the pitiless winds claw my sides,
>> and dig deep holes upon my face.

> Lord,
>> When I think I am deep,
>> like the untroubled depths of the sea,
>> I lose myself in shallows,
>> and my energy in restless foam.
>> Each tide of effort retreats from the shore
>> with a murmur of futility, a sigh of despair.

>> I see all my life
>> as a frieze of moods
>> like the moods of the sea—
>> grey moods of coldness,
>> moods, coloured moods—

24

and thoughts like spray.
All my attempts to be creative
end in the building of bubbles, bright bubbles
like the breeze-blown bubbles
from the crest of a wave.

God's purpose in the Cross was to bring us out of the futility of meaningless existence, to redeem us. And He comes to us with the question, What are you doing with your life ? Are you drifting at the mercy of every wind of thought and rumour ? Or have you a foundation laid upon a rock ?

The great Christians who faced persecution and death for their faith did so because God had delivered them from the happy-go-lucky drift of aimlessness into the discipline and strength of His control. Such a man was Nicholas Ridley. He had a vivid and eventful career. At the age of twenty-six he took his Cambridge M.A., and after studying in Paris he returned to Cambridge. He became one of the university proctors in 1534 and signed the decree of the university against the jurisdiction of the Pope in England. Three years later he was chaplain to Cranmer, Archbishop of Canterbury, and many appointments followed. In the momentous year 1548 he went as Bishop of Rochester along with other visitors nominated to establish Protestantism in Cambridge University, and in the same year he helped to compile the *Book of Common Prayer* which, in 1949, was four-hundred years old.

The following year he examined the Catholic Bishops Gardiner and Bonner. They were deprived of their bishoprics and Ridley followed Bonner as Bishop of London. He signed the papers which settled the English crown on Lady Jane Grey and declared Mary and

Elizabeth to be illegitimate. In agreeing to the statement that the succession of Mary to the throne would be a disaster to English religious interests he laid up trouble for himself, for when Mary did come to power, though Ridley asked her pardon, he was arrested and imprisoned in the Tower of London. Here he continued to write in defence of his faith until with Latimer he was sent to Oxford for his trial. He was excommunicated and returned to prison, but a year later new penal laws were enacted, he was retried, sentenced, and publicly burnt to death in the street near Balliol College.

To the end he acted with courage. He and Latimer were marched to the stake, Ridley dressed in a black furred gown such as were then worn by bishops. A sermon was preached to him, though he was not allowed to reply ; then he gave most of his clothes to people in the crowd and was fastened to the stake by an iron chain. He appealed to the Queen's Commissioner to care for some poor dependants of his and the faggots at his feet were lit. One of the most famous sentences in the English language is the message of good cheer which Latimer spoke to Ridley at that moment : ' We shall this day light such a candle by God's grace in England as, I trust, shall never be put out.' Latimer was overcome by the fire almost immediately, but Ridley endured frightful pain before he was released by death.

AN ACT OF DEVOTION

A Prayer

Here is a prayer of Nicholas Ridley, written in 1555, the year of his martyrdom :

O heavenly Father, the Father of all wisdom, understanding, and true strength, I beseech Thee, look mercifully upon me, and send Thy Holy Spirit into my breast ; that when I must join to fight in the field for the glory of Thy Holy Name, then I, being strengthened with the defence of Thy right hand, may manfully stand in the confession of Thy faith, and of Thy truth, and continue in the same unto the end of my life, through our Lord Jesus Christ.   Amen.

A hymn of Johann Winckler (*M.H.B.*, No. 783) translated by John Wesley expresses the mood of Ridley's prayer :

> Shall I, for fear of feeble man,
> The Spirit's course in me restrain ?
> Or, undismayed, in deed and word
> Be a true witness for my Lord ?
>
> Saviour of men, Thy searching eye
> Doth all my inmost thoughts descry ;
> Doth aught on earth my wishes raise,
> Or the world's pleasures or its praise ?
>
> The love of Christ doth me constrain
> To seek the wandering souls of men ;
> With cries, entreaties, tears, to save,
> To snatch them from the gaping grave.
>
> My life, my blood, I here present,
> If for Thy truth they may be spent :
> Fulfil Thy sovereign counsel, Lord ;
> Thy will be done, Thy name adored.
>
> Give me Thy strength, O God of power ;
> Then, let winds blow or thunders roar,
> Thy faithful witness will I be :
> 'Tis fixed : I can do all through Thee !

THE PURPOSE OF OUR LIVES

One of the most impressive facts about the world of today is the way God has prepared his Church in various countries to meet the demands of contemporary life. This is seen very clearly in South India, where twenty-five years of prayer, discussion, and study recently culminated in the union of the Churches. Many of us grew impatient while negotiations were going on and asked whether it needed a quarter of a century of debate before such a union could be consummated. But God united His Church in South India in the very year when India herself fell apart ; when Hindus and Muslims set up separate dominions and millions of people died in the communal riots that resulted from the division. As a symbol of this unity of the Church in the conflict of the State, there comes the story of how in one place during the rioting the Muslims and the Hindus both put their women and children over the wall of the Christian compound each night as it fell dark while they went on with the fighting. India, the land which really loves unity, cannot fail to be impressed by the new fellowship within the Christian community.

In China, God has been preparing, through years of tumult and chaos, a Church led by the Chinese themselves, so that when the curtain comes down upon that country, and if it becomes difficult for the Church in Europe and America to keep in touch with Chinese Christians, they are trained and ready to accept responsibility, able to take decisions and willing to bear the burden of ordering the finances of the Church. It was not always like that ; in fact it is only in recent years that these lessons have been learned. Missionaries in China used to reckon that they had not only to speak Chinese, but to think Chinese. It is said that one missionary had trouble with the staff of a school and was visited by a member of his church, who in true Chinese fashion talked about nothing in particular for an hour or so, and then, as he was going said : ' Oh, by the way, about the trouble at the school. Whatever you do, don't dismiss the head master.' The missionary thought it over, wondering why that last sentence had been said, and then, next morning, went out and dismissed the head master. In a few hours the church member was back again saying : ' You're the first missionary that understands plain Chinese.' That was a few years ago, but today it is a different story. The Chinese have learnt to speak their mind and to stand by their decisions. Much of the recent U.N.R.R.A. relief was dispensed by Chinese ministers. This is revolutionary in China : Confucius himself said that it is difficult to dispense charity, meaning that you please no one by doing so, for every one thinks that he has had a smaller share than others, and that the one in charge is keeping his own rake-off. In one province only one Chinese minister came under suspicion for not having distributed the benefits fairly. He was found to have acted foolishly rather than corruptly, and it was his own Chinese colleagues who took the disciplinary action. This is the Church, equipped with Chinese ministers, teachers, doctors, and nurses, that God has prepared to carry on His work in China.

The story of Nathaniel Gilbert shows how in the West Indies the Church was *inside* slavery before emancipation. That is why, in British islands, the slaves went to the churches to give thanks on the night of their liberation— in some other islands, French and Dutch, they turned upon their former owners and murdered those they hated. But it is well known now that the Negroes of the West Indies were set free to continue in misery, in poverty and immorality, so that today their descendants live in some of the poorest houses in the world and three quarters of their children are born outside marriage. A new emancipation is planned for these people ; liberty from want and rotten home life. Within this plan it is to the Church that men look for the people to transform men's lives. The State can grant money, and it can rebuild property, but it cannot change houses into homes. The Church, inside the life of the people is ready for this new act of emancipation.

So God has prepared His Church ; a tool forged and tempered for special tasks. We may well turn to ask what He has prepared *us* for. Not merely, what has He trained and moulded His Church in Britain to face, though that would be a searching question to ask ; but, more personally, what has He been preparing you and me for ? And let us ask the bigger question first. What is He preparing us for in terms of eternity ?

We sometimes lose sight of the vastness of eternity, beside which the span of our mortal life is microscopically brief, just as we tend to forget how small is our size compared with the vast spaces of the universe. We belong to a group of planets spinning round the sun. The light which comes to us, ninety-three million miles from the sun, travels at 186,000 miles a second and reaches us in about eight minutes. The light from the most distant galaxy that has been discovered has been travelling at the same rate for one hundred and fifty million years. A galaxy is a group of stars each of which is something like our sun. It takes a hundred thousand million stars to make one galaxy, and there are a hundred thousand million galaxies in the universe.

> When I consider Thy heavens,
> The work of Thy fingers,
> The moon and the stars which Thou hast ordained ;
> What is man, that Thou art mindful of him ?
> And the son of man, that Thou visitest him ?
> For Thou hast made him but little lower than God,
> And crownest him with glory and honour.

What for ? What is the purpose of our lives, laid as they are in such an infinite setting ? The acquirement of skill at table-tennis ? To provide opportunities for knitting, going to the cinema, listening to the Light Programme and filling up football pools ? Could we possibly face an eternity of activities like these ?

Or, to come down to everyday life, what is God's purpose for our lives in the coming days and months which may remain to us ? What is God preparing you and me for in the next ten years ? And how are we preparing to serve His purpose ?

Let us be clear about one fact. We can have nothing to offer in God's Name to our day and generation ; nothing really important to say to the group to which we belong—family or Youth Club or cricket team ; nothing to tell society about God and eternity, unless from time to time we withdraw from the group and from society to a place of prayer and study and worship. Nor can we expect to withstand any time of storm unless we have prepared for it in calm weather. An old Scotch shepherd when he was dying was asked whether he would like to have a passage from the Bible read to him, and he said : ' No, I thatched my house in fair weather.' It is in that confident spirit of those who have been prepared by the Word of God, not in any confidence of their own, that men like Ridley stood firm in times of trial.

Some time ago, when the Methodist Forward Movement flourished, there appeared in the *Recorder* an announcement that the Forward Movement would hold a Retreat. Many of us laughed at the time, but that is the only way to hold a forward movement in the Church. The true Christian retreat is not the quivering refuge of the terror-stricken disciples on the day after Good Friday, nor the cave of Elijah on Horeb, but a place of quietness in which to receive equipment for the conflict. It is the place of confidence where we get ready for the onslaught of doubt ; the time of worship when we encounter God and receive the strength to meet the coming day.

A Norwegian woman, when she was asked if she did not find the long dark winter trying replied : ' There is always an hour of daylight in which to prepare the lamps.' That is one of the functions of worship, to draw us apart for study and devotion so that we may know how to stand when difficulties come upon us.

Indians say that in the winter, when the crocodile goes to sleep, it is kept from feeling hungry by a stone in its stomach. Small, hard, compact, of definite shape resisting all attempts to digest it and to take it up into the rest of the body, the stone continues to be itself, unchanged. The Church in the world is like that. Unbending and uncompromising, it is there as a hard kernel, serving the rest but not becoming so much a part of society that its identity and its distinctive character are lost. It is the place where God does His work in His world, and it is made up of people like you and me, so the same firm stand must be seen in our lives too.

The rhythm of withdrawal, for worship and study, and return, to the life of conflict and witness, is typical of the life of the Christian disciple. It is seen in the life of the great reformer John Huss who was martyred in Czecho-slovakia during the year 1415. He was known for his bold, outspoken way of witnessing to his beliefs, so that it was particularly significant when his statue in Prague was found gagged one morning after the Communists had taken over. Huss was the chief link between Wyclif and Luther in handing on the flame that kindled the Reformation and like Ridley he was burnt for his uncompromising faith. While the faggots were being piled around him he said : ' God is my witness that I have never taught or preached that which false witnesses have testified against me. He knows that the great object of all my preaching and writing was to convert men from sin. In the truth of that gospel which hitherto I have written, taught and preached, I now joyfully die.'

On this day when we recall the time when the disciples were in despair and Jesus still lay in the tomb, let us remember men like John Huss and Nicholas Ridley who retained their faith through all that opposition could inflict, and let us recollect the words of the prisoner St. Paul :[1]

THE WORD OF GOD IS NOT BOUND

Charles Wesley has given us a hymn (*M.H.B.*, No. 465) which takes up the ideas of withdrawal to encounter God, to learn the meaning of the Cross of Christ, and return to life that is lived in Him :

> Open, Lord, my inward ear,
> And bid my heart rejoice ;

[1] 2 Timothy 2⁹.

Bid my quiet spirit hear
    Thy comfortable voice ;
Never in the whirlwind found,
    Or where earthquakes rock the place,
Still and silent is the sound,
    The whisper of Thy grace.

From the world of sin, and noise,
    And hurry I withdraw ;
For the small and inward voice
    I wait with humble awe ;
Silent am I now and still,
    Dare not in Thy presence move ;
To my waiting soul reveal
    The secret of Thy love.

Thou didst undertake for me,
    For me to death wast sold ;
Wisdom in a mystery
    Of bleeding love unfold ;
Teach the lesson of Thy Cross,
    Let me die with Thee to reign ;
All things let me count but loss,
    So I may Thee regain.

Show me, as my soul can bear,
    The depth of inbred sin ;
All the unbelief declare,
    The pride that lurks within ;
Take me, whom Thyself hast bought,
    Bring into captivity
Every high aspiring thought
    That would not stoop to Thee.

Lord, my time is in Thy hand,
    My soul to Thee convert ;
Thou canst make me understand,

Though I am slow of heart ;
Thine in whom I live and move,
Thine the work, the praise is Thine ;
Thou art wisdom, power, and love,
And all Thou art is mine.   Amen.

An Act of Thanksgiving (from the Covenant Service)

MINISTER :

Let us rise and give thanks to God for His manifold mercies.

O God our Father, the fountain of all goodness, who hast been gracious to us through all the years of our life : we give Thee thanks for Thy loving-kindness which has filled our days and brought us to this time and place.

PEOPLE :

We praise Thy holy Name, O Lord.

MINISTER :

Thou hast given us life and reason, and set us in a world which is full of Thy glory.   Thou hast comforted us with kindred and friends, and ministered to us through the hands and minds of our fellows.

PEOPLE :

We praise Thy holy Name, O Lord.

MINISTER :

Thou hast set in our hearts a hunger for Thee, and given us Thy peace.   Thou hast redeemed us and called us to a high calling in Christ Jesus.   Thou hast given us a place in the fellowship of Thy Spirit and the witness of Thy Church.

PEOPLE :

We praise Thy holy Name, O Lord.

MINISTER :

In darkness Thou hast been our light ; in adversity and temptation a rock of strength ; in our joys the very spirit of joy ; in our labours the all-sufficient reward.

PEOPLE :

We praise Thy holy Name, O Lord.

MINISTER :

Thou hast remembered us when we have forgotten Thee, followed us even when we fled from Thee, met us with forgiveness when we turned back to Thee. For all Thy long-suffering and the abundance of Thy grace,

PEOPLE :

We praise Thy holy Name, O Lord.

A Prayer (The Collect for the Sunday next before Easter from the Prayer Book of Latimer and Ridley) :

Almighty and everlasting God, Who, of Thy tender love toward mankind, hast sent Thy Son, our Saviour Jesus Christ, to take upon Him our flesh, and to suffer death upon the Cross, that all mankind should follow the example of His great humility ; Mercifully grant, that we may both follow the example of His patience, and also be made partakers of His resurrection ; through the same Jesus Christ our Lord. Amen.

EASTER DAY

Where Are You Going?

IT is said that during the persecution of the Christians under Nero, Paul and Peter were thrown into prison in Rome. The Christians in Rome pressed Peter to escape so that he could continue his leadership of the Church in some other part of the world. In the end he acted upon the suggestion and, in some way not told in the story, he was able to get away from the prison and made his way to the city gate. Just as he was going to pass through to the freedom beyond, he was halted by a Vision. There was no mistaking the form of Jesus, and Peter cried : ' Lord, whither goest Thou ? ' The Vision answered : ' I am come to Rome to be crucified a second time.' That was enough for Peter and he returned, ashamed, to be crucified himself, upside-down, at his own request, for he could not bear the thought of being crucified in the same position as his Lord.

That is the well-known ' *Quo Vadis* ' legend, and some have suggested that it may be a displaced Resurrection story ; that it may have occurred in Jerusalem to Peter escaping to Galilee after the crucifixion. Whether there is any historical truth in the story or not, it is true to the character of Jesus. We find the Risen Lord with the same personality as the Jesus of Nazareth : He certainly appeared to Peter, even if not in the manner of the legend, and, from desperate misery because of the denial, He led him to hope and made him a man of courage ; He came to Mary, who had been demented by her loss of Him, and calmed her troubled mind ; He joined the two who were walking at evening-time and changed their numb despair to gladness. This was the same Jesus that men knew in Galilee, and He is at work in the world today.

If we were to ask Him now, ' Whither goest Thou ? ', would He answer again : ' To be crucified a second time by the sin and folly of men ' ? Is that what we have done to Him by our atom bombs and concentration camps, and by our selfishness and indifference to Him ? Would he say again that He was going to His Church in her trouble ? —that wherever men still suffer for their faith and are loyal to Him in the time of trial He is there ? Or would He say that He was going to reign eternally from the Cross ?

The earliest Christian paintings do not show Christ as *suffering* upon the Cross. One reason was that they had a deep and awful reverence for Christ as God coupled with the conviction that He was risen, alive for evermore and present with them ; and in the second place, they found it hard to answer the taunt of the heathen that they worshipped a crucified man. The heathen would not easily understand the answer offered by St. Augustine : ' The Son of Man was crucified, not that the Cross should disgrace Christ, but that by the Sacrament of Christ the Cross should become the ensign of our victory.' Even up to the tenth century the Crucifix as we know it had not appeared, and the Crucified Christ was represented in long robes, crowned, majestic and with open eyes. The idea was always in accordance with the old rendering of Psalm 96[10] : *Regnavit e ligno*— The Lord *reign from the tree*. So that if the answer to the question, ' Lord, whither goest Thou ? ', is, ' To be crucified a second time,' let us beware of offering our pity.

' Daughters of Jerusalem,' said Jesus on his way to the Cross, ' weep not for me, but weep for yourselves and your children.'

> Weep not for Him who onward bears
> His Cross to Calvary ;
> He does not ask man's pitying tears,
> Who wills for man to die.

Throughout the New Testament the writers seem impatient of lingering for a moment on the idea of Christ as dead. ' He died for our sins—and rose again for our justification.' ' It is Christ that died—yea, rather that is risen again.'

But suppose the question be turned upon us, and Christ should say to us : ' Where are you going ? ' The message of Easter is that in Christ we have the answer to man's ancient questions about his life after death.

The Venerable Bede lived in the late seventh and early eighth centuries. Almost all we know about him is from a short autobiography at the end of his *Ecclesiastical History of England*—the book which makes him the Father of English history. He had a most uneventful life, almost entirely lived near Jarrow, though he visited Lindisfarne before 721—did he see the *Lindisfarne Gospels* being written ?—and York in 733. At the age of seven he was handed over to the care of the Abbots of Jarrow and Wearmouth, and as he says : ' From that time I have spent the whole of my life within that monastery, devoting all my pains to the study of the scriptures ; and amid the observance of monastic discipline, and the daily charge of singing in the church, it has ever been my delight to learn or teach or write.' One of the most familiar stories in our history is the account of how he spent his last moments finishing the translation of St. John's Gospel. In his *Ecclesiastical History*, Bede tells the story of how Paulinus came preaching to Edwin of Northumbria. At the Council held in A.D. 627, Coifi, the high priest of Odin in Yorkshire rode out to overthrow the shrine it was his duty to guard, with the remark that the old religion obviously had no virtue in it because no one had applied himself more diligently to the worship of the gods than he had done, yet he had never got anything out of it. Another of the King's men approved the new religion on a much higher level in the words :

The present life of man, O king, seems to me, in comparison of that time which is unknown to us, like to the swift flight of a sparrow through the room wherein you sit at supper in winter, with your commanders and ministers, and a good fire in the midst, whilst the storms of rain and snow prevail abroad ; the sparrow, I say, flying in at one door, and immediately out at another, whilst he is within, is safe from the wintry storm ; but after a short space of fair weather, he immediately vanishes out of your sight, into the dark winter from which he had emerged. So this life of man appears for a short space, but of what went before, or what is to follow, we are utterly ignorant. If, therefore, this new doctrine contains something more certain, it seems justly to deserve to be followed.

AN ACT OF DEVOTION

A hymn by Phillip Doddridge (M.H.B., No. 217) combines the ideas of the Resurrection of Christ—His eternal victory and reign, and the everlasting life offered by God to man :

Ye humble souls that seek the Lord,
    Chase all your fears away ;
And bow with rapture down to see
    The place where Jesus lay.

Thus low the Lord of Life was brought,
    Such wonders love can do ;
Thus cold in death that bosom lay,
    Which throbbed and bled for you.

But raise your eyes and tune your songs ;
    The Saviour lives again :
Not all the bolts and bars of death
    The Conqueror could detain.

High o'er the angelic bands He rears
    His once dishonoured head ;
And through unnumbered years He reigns,
    Who dwelt among the dead.

With joy like His shall every saint
    His vacant tomb survey ;
Then rise with his ascending Lord
    To realms of endless day.

The Reading

St. Mark's Gospel ends in the middle of a sentence. No
one knows whether the end of the papyrus roll it was
written on was carelessly torn, or whether the writer was
interrupted in his work and never finished it, but the story
ends abruptly with these words :

And when the sabbath was past, Mary Magdalene,
and Mary the mother of James, and Salome, bought
spices, that they might come and anoint him. And
very early on the first day of the week, they come to
the tomb when the sun was risen. And they were

saying among themselves, Who shall roll us away the stone from the door of the tomb ? and looking up, they see that the stone is rolled back : for it was exceeding great. And entering into the tomb, they saw a young man sitting on the right side, arrayed in a white robe ; and they were amazed. And he saith unto them, Be not amazed : ye seek Jesus, the Nazarene, which hath been crucified : he is risen ; he is not here : behold, the place where they laid him ! But go, tell his disciples and Peter, He goeth before you into Galilee : there shall ye see him, as he said unto you. And they went out, and fled from the tomb ; for trembling and astonishment had come upon them : and they said nothing to any one ; for they were afraid. . . . (Mark 16¹⁻⁸. The rest of this chapter was added later.).

The Prayer
The Collect for Easter Day

Almighty God, who through Thine only-begotten Son Jesus Christ hast overcome death, and opened unto us the gate of everlasting life ; We humbly beseech Thee, that, as by Thy special grace preventing us Thou dost put into our minds good desires, so by Thy continual help we may bring the same to good effect ; through Jesus Christ our Lord, who liveth and reigneth with Thee and the Holy Ghost, ever one God, world without end. Amen.

RESURGAM

On the morning after a heavy raid there was placed over the door of a blitzed church in Plymouth the one word : RESURGAM—I will arise again. The wood-work was still smouldering and the debris had not been cleared ; yet the prophecy was no idle boast and soon the assurance of its truth was seen in the clearing of the site, the erecting of an altar and pulpit open to the vault of heaven and the planting of lawns and flower beds in the nave. Since then regular open-air services have been held within the roofless walls and in a very real sense a strong living Church has arisen upon the ashes of destruction. No doubt some day the work of reconstruction will begin and in the architectural sense the prophecy, ' I will arise again,' will be fulfilled, but whether that happens or not, the claim behind that word *Resurgam* has been upheld: there was life in that Church which would not be denied and the gates of hell could not prevail against it.

Jesus once said : ' Destroy this temple, and in three days I will raise it up.'[1] He spoke of His Risen Body, which after the Ascension and Pentecost is to be found in the Church, the 'holy temple in the Lord, in whom ye also are builded together for a habitation of God in the Spirit.'[2] The Jews believed that the Temple was the habitation of God ; Jesus says that His Body, which is to be raised up after His death, will be the dwelling-place of God among men—His Body of which we are members. The fulfilment of this prophecy is the proof of the Resurrection.

If Jesus had not been raised from the dead, there would have been no Christian Church, no New Testament and no change of the day of worship from the Sabbath to the first day of the week. No Jew would have conceived it possible to change the day of worship, but for this one reason that it was on the first that Jesus returned to his disciples and brought them victory in what had seemed defeat. Now they could go and *do* something about the

[1] John 2[10].　　[2] Ephesians 2[21-2].

problems of sin and suffering and death. They had seen the strong hands of God twist a crown of thorns into a crown of glory, and in such hands they knew that they were safe. While he had lived with them they had misunderstood nearly everything he had said to them, but now it all made sense at last. And from now on, the day which saw Him rise, which felt the resurge of hope and life into their views, became the day which they set apart for worship.

If Jesus had not been raised from the dead there would have been no New Testament. No one would have troubled to have written the book if Jesus had finished as a condemned and crucified revolutionary. You don't go home and write up the full account of the defeat of your team ; nations erect no monuments and carve no inscriptions extolling the deeds of their soldiers in the battles they have lost. No one would have had cause or impulse to write the story of the vanquished Jesus : but the message that Christ was victorious over death *had* to be written ; when it became clear that His coming again was delayed it would have been criminal negligence not to record the facts for all to read. An early picture of Calvary shows the two robbers on the crosses, but in the centre, instead of a representation of the crucifixion there is a cross in leaf and bloom ! Not a piece of dead wood, but a symbol of returning life. It was that new life that expressed itself in the early Church and provided the energy for the writing of the New Testament.

The most convincing proof of the fact of the resurrection always has been and still is the fact of the existence of the Church. It isn't merely that in towns and villages all over the world there are Churches where men and women worship Jesus Christ as Lord. It is the people who form the Church who are the final proof. The word *Resurgam* reminds us of those words in the Vulgate version of the story of the Prodigal Son : *surgam, et ibo ad patrem meum*— I will arise and go to my father.[3] This is the true resurrection, the true renewal of life. As the father said to the servants when he told them to bring out the best robe and put it on the returned prodigal, and to put a ring on his hand, and shoes on his feet : ' For this my son was dead, and is alive again ; he was lost and is found.' This is what Paul had in mind when he prayed : ' That I might know him, and the power of his resurrection.'[4]

Thornton Wilder has given us a fascinating story in his *Bridge of San Luis Rey*. He tells how at noon on a day in the early eighteenth century, the finest bridge in all Peru broke and threw five travellers into the gulf below. The bridge was a show-piece for every visitor. It had been woven of willow wands by the Incas, and it spanned a gap across a deep rift in the high road between Lima and Cuzco. For over a century hundreds of people had passed over it daily, and it looked as though it would last for ever. After the tragedy, a memorial service was held in the Cathedral, and since everyone in the city used the bridge at some time or other, and any one of them might have been among the victims, there was great searching of heart in Lima. Servant girls returned the jewellery they had stolen from their mistresses, money-lenders argued angrily with their wives in defence of usury. Everybody was deeply impressed, but only one person did anything about it. He was brother Juniper, a Roman Catholic priest who had been sent as a missionary to Peru from Northern Italy. The red-haired little Franiscan saw the tragedy, and he spent the next six years investigating

[3] Luke 15[18].   [4] Philippians 3[10].

45

the lives of the five who had died. He knocked on all the doors in the city and asked endless questions in his attempt to show that each life was a perfect whole. What he did show was that each of those lives was inextricably woven into the texture of the others and that, as if by some overriding power, they were focused upon that moment of the collapsing bridge. The lives of those five travellers converged upon that bridge of destruction : ours converge upon the Cross and Resurrection of Jesus, the bridge of life : 'for God sent not His Son into the world to condemn the world ; but that the world through Him might be saved.'[5] For Peter, restored from weakness to strength, for Mary Magdalene brought back from insanity to health, for Thomas reclaimed from doubt to certainty, the bridge was Faith, built by God, that took them from death to life. Their faith was in the Death and Resurrection of Jesus.

That is why the symbol of Christianity is neither a crucifix nor the empty tomb. Not a crucifix, because that only represents half the victory of God. It is not a mere idle twist of words to speak about the victory of the Cross, for there is the stern reality of the victory of undeviating purpose and unshaken love, the triumph over man's enemies. As Saint Paul put it,[6] God cancelled the deed that excluded us from the inheritance and made it of no importance, nailing it to the Cross. In Christ, God robbed of their prey all the forces arrayed against us, putting them to open shame by leading them in triumph as a Roman Emperor exhibited his captives.

Nor is the Christian symbol the empty tomb, though it represents the other half of the victory of God. If Jesus had merely been God living with us for a time, and if he had died and returned to His Father without facing the Cross, He would have been to us an impossible example and a mockery of our finer aspirations. But when the two are taken together, Crucifixion and Resurrection, as symbolized in the empty cross, we have the power to make the example possible and our hopes for ourselves can be fulfilled. The story of Easter Day then becomes more than what H. G. Wells thought it to be ; the conventional happy ending to the tragedy of Good Friday. It is part of the Act of God on behalf of man ; it is the assurance that Christ has conquered death for us.

> With joy like His shall every saint
> His vacant tomb survey.

Thy symbol of the empty Cross speaks to us of hope, of unconquerable life, of unquenchable faith. It reminds us of the words of St. John that whatever originates from God is certain to triumph over the world,[7] and then he goes on to make that great affirmation :

THIS IS THE VICTORY THAT OVERCOMETH THE
WORLD, EVEN OUR FAITH.

A hymn by the French writer Edmond Louis Budry (*H.M.B.*, No. 213), translated by Richard Birch Hoyle reminds us that through our faith in the Resurrection of Jesus we are made ' more than conquerors '[8] over the trials and distresses of this life :

Thine be the glory, risen, conquering Son,
Endless is the victory Thou o'er death hast won ;
Angels in bright raiment rolled the stone away,
Kept the folded grave-clothes, where Thy body lay.

[7] 1 John 5[4].   [8] Romans 8[37].

47

Lo ! Jesus meets us, risen from the tomb ;
Lovingly He greets us, scatters fear and gloom ;
Let the Church with gladness, hymns of triumph sing,
For her Lord now liveth, death hath lost its sting.

No more we doubt Thee, glorious Prince of life ;
Life is nought without Thee : aid us in our strife ;
Make us more than conquerors, through Thy deathless love :
Bring us safe through Jordan to Thy home above.

An act of Confession (from the Covenant Service)

MINISTER :

Let us now examine ourselves before God, humbly
confessing our sins and watching our hearts, lest by
self-deceit we shut ourselves out from His presence.
Let us pray.

O God our Father, who hast set forth the way of life
for us in Thy beloved Son : we confess with shame
our slowness to learn of Him, our reluctance to
follow Him. Thou hast spoken and called, and we
have not given heed ; Thy beauty has shone forth
and we have been blind ; Thou hast stretched out
Thy hands to us through our fellows and we have
passed by. We have taken great benefits with little
thanks ; we have been unworthy of Thy changeless
love.

PEOPLE :

Have mercy upon us and forgive us, O Lord.

MINISTER :

Forgive us, we beseech Thee, the poverty of our worship,
the formality and selfishness of our prayers, our
inconstancy and unbelief, our neglect of fellowship
and of the means of grace, our hesitating witness for
Christ, our false pretences and our wilful ignorance
of Thy ways.

PEOPLE :
Have mercy upon us and forgive us, O Lord.

MINISTER :
Forgive us wherein we have wasted our time or misused our gifts. Forgive us wherein we have excused our own wrong-doing or evaded our responsibilities. Forgive us that we have been unwilling to overcome evil with good, that we have drawn back from the Cross.

PEOPLE :
Have mercy upon us and forgive us, O Lord.

MINISTER :
Forgive us that so little of Thy love has reached others through us, and that we have borne so lightly wrongs and sufferings that were not our own. Forgive us wherein we have cherished the things that divide us from others, and wherein we have made it hard for them to live with us ; And wherein we have been thoughtless in our judgements, hasty in condemnation, grudging in forgiveness.

PEOPLE :
Have mercy upon us and forgive us, O Lord.

MINISTER :
If we have made no ventures in fellowship ; if we have kept in our heart a grievance against another ; if we have not sought reconciliation ; if we have been eager for the punishment of wrong-doers, and slow to seek their redemption ;

PEOPLE :
Have mercy upon us and forgive us, O Lord.

MINISTER :
Let each of us in silence make confession to God.

After a period of Silent Prayer the Minister and People shall say,

Have mercy upon me, O God, according to Thy loving-kindness ; according to the multitude of Thy tender mercies, blot out my transgressions. Wash me throughly from mine iniquity, and cleanse me from my sin. Create in me a clean heart, O God, and renew a right spirit within me.

Then, the People still kneeling, the Minister shall rise and say,

This is the message which we have heard from Him, and declare unto you, that God is Light, and in Him is no darkness at all. If we walk in the light, as He is in the light, we have fellowship one with another, and the blood of Jesus His Son cleanseth us from all sin. If we say that we have no sin, we deceive ourselves, and the truth is not in us. If we confess our sins, He is faithful and righteous to forgive us our sins, and to cleanse us from all unrighteousness. Amen.

EASTER MONDAY

What is That in Your Hand?

WHEN any man is called by God to a special task
his first thought is, Why me ? What have I to
offer in this service ? It was true of the great Old
Testament prophets : Isaiah's response to the Vision of
God was to say : ' Woe is me ! for I am undone ; because
I am a man of unclean lips, and I dwell in the midst of
a people of unclean lips : for mine eyes have seen the
King, the Lord of hosts.' [1] Jeremiah, the youth who was
called to be a prophet to the nations, replied immediately :
' Ah, Lord God ! behold I cannot speak : for I am
a child.' [2]

But the prophets did not rest there. Humble as they
were about their own ability and equipment, knowing
that they were not good enough for the service of the
Holy God, they had heard a call that could not be denied
and they went out to work in reliance upon God and in
the faith that He had touched their lips and made them
clean.

The first of them all, Moses, was the most sure of his
own weakness and limitations and the story of his call is
the story of how God had to show him that men would
listen when he made the amazing claim that he came to
them with a message from God.

And Moses said unto God, Who am I, that I should
go unto Pharaoh, and that I should bring forth the
children of Israel out of Egypt ? And he said,

[1] Isaiah 6⁵.　　　[2] Jeremiah 1⁶.

Certainly I will be with thee ; and this shall be the token unto thee, that I have sent thee : when thou hast brought forth the people out of Egypt, ye shall serve God upon this mountain. And Moses said unto God, Behold, when I come unto the children of Israel, and shall say unto them, The God of your fathers hath sent me unto you ; and they shall say to me, What is his name ? what shall I say unto them ? And God said unto Moses, I AM THAT I AM : and he said, Thus shalt thou say unto the children of Israel, I AM hath sent me unto you. . . . And Moses answered and said, But, behold, they will not believe me, nor hearken unto my voice : for they will say, The Lord hath not appeared unto thee. And the Lord said unto him, What is that in thine hand ? And he said, A rod. And he said, Cast it on the ground. And he cast it on the ground, and it became a serpent ; and Moses fled from before it. And the Lord said unto Moses, Put forth thine hand, and take it by the tail : (and he put forth his hand, and laid hold of it, and it became a rod in his hand :) that they may believe that the Lord, the God of their fathers, the God of Abraham, the God of Isaac, and the God of Jacob, hath appeared unto thee. (Exodus 3^{11-14} ; 4^{1-5}.)

When Deaville Walker retired from his work as editor to the Methodist Missionary Society, he told for the first time the story of the secret behind the high standard of photography which had made the *Kingdom Overseas* outstanding among missionary publications.

As a boy of sixteen he was asked by his father what he would like for his birthday. When he said he would like a camera, his father replied that if that was his choice he should have the best camera available, one that would last a lifetime. Soon the boy found that by taking photographs of his friends at school he could make his camera a source of profit and it brought him a useful income. One Sunday night he was present when a preacher chose as his text the words of God to Moses: ' What is that in thine hand ? ', and, as was the custom of preachers in those days, he kept repeating the text, thrusting the question forward, and at the end, when it came for the last time, ' What is that in thine hand ? ', the boy answered : ' It's my camera, Lord.'

From that time onward the camera was dedicated to the service of God. The time came when it went with Deaville Walker all over the world, to every station of the missionary society in those days, and everywhere it took photographs which have told the Home Church the story of the triumphs and needs of the Church overseas. The secret was in the answer of that boy to the question, What is that in thine hand ?

> Let the boy play here,
>   Mary my wife ;
> Nails are good toys for him,
>   Mary my own.
> Tools are beyond his reach ;
> Later their use I'll teach :
>   Nails cannot hurt him.
>
> Lay the boy by the bench,
>   Mary my wife ;
> See how he grasps the wood,
>   Mary my own.
> Look at the cross he's made—
> He'll quickly learn the trade.
>   Wood cannot hurt him.
>
> Leave your high dreams of him,
>   Mary my wife ;

Flesh of my flesh is he.
　　Mary my own.
Woodworker's son is he:
Woodworker will he be,
　　Nails in his hands.

He'll be a carpenter,
　　Mary my wife,
Just like his father is,
　　Mary my own:
Woodwork his daily bread,
Woodwork his dying bed—
　　Nails in his hands.[1]

Does Cologne mean anything more to you than eau de Cologne? There is the cathedral, of course, unique in that though it took five hundred years to build it was finished to the original design; but Cologne means more to us than that: it is linked with a more lasting and grander achievement than the Cathedral—the English Bible. In 1524 William Tyndale went to settle there. He had tried to work at the translation of the New Testament while living in London, but he had been driven out by the combined forces of Church and State.

He was a country lad, educated at Oxford and Cambridge. It was in Cambridge that he came to know the new learning, and acquired the scholarship that prepared him for the task of translation. If Tyndale had been asked, ' What is that in thine hand?', he might have replied, ' A pen, Lord,' and there is no doubt that his pen was dedicated to the service of God. He became tutor to a wealthy family in the Cotswolds, and was so disgusted at the ignorance of the clergy he met in his master's house, that he determined to make it possible for

[1] Poem by Donald S. Ching.

anyone to know more about the Bible than they did. He set out to translate the New Testament into plain English so that ' a boy that driveth the plough ' could understand it. He hoped for help from the Bishop of London, but he was met with hostility, and it soon became necessary for him to leave the country. He settled at Cologne, and had made some progress with the printing when he was found by an English spy. The Dean of Frankfurt warned the Cologne authorities against him and the message was sent to Henry the Eighth and Wolsey to watch the English ports for copies of the Book. He escaped to Worms with some of the sheets, and there he published a complete translation. Copies were brought into England by stealth, surely one of the most glorious pieces of smuggling in history. Wherever they were found the volumes were suppressed and the Archbishop of Canterbury had agents on the continent buying all they could find. Another attempt was made to capture Tyndale and he escaped to Marburg. Henry the Eighth demanded that the Emperor of the Netherlands should hand him over ' as one who was spreading sedition in England.' The end came in 1535 when Tyndale was betrayed by one he had befriended ; he was seized and imprisoned in the castle of Vilvorde. A year later, to quote *Foxe's Martyrs*,

he was brought forth to the place of execution, was there tied to the stake, and there strangled first by the hangman, and afterwards by fire consumed . . . crying thus at the stake, with a fervent zeal and a loud voice : 'Lord, open the King of England's eyes.'

This was the man who laid the foundation of the Authorized Version of the New Testament, as is acknowledged in the Reviser's Preface to the New Testament.

In hardship and poverty, hunted and in danger of his life he applied himself to the most careful scrutiny of the Greek documents and to the strictest accuracy in his translation, making a revision of his work which led Westcott, one of the great Cambridge scholars who helped in preparing the Revised Version, to wonder at the very minuteness of the changes which he made. Such was the diligence of the man, who, with a price on his head, wrote of his revised edition of 1534.

My part be not in Christ if mine heart be not to follow and live according as I teach, and also if mine heart weep not night and day for mine own sin and other men's indifferently, beseeching God to convert us all and to take His wrath from us and to be merciful as well to all other men, as to mine own soul. . . . As concerning all I have translated or otherwise written, I beseech all men to read it for that purpose I wrote it, even to bring them to the knowledge of the Scripture.

AN ACT OF DEVOTION

The Reading

Here is part of St. John's Gospel in Tyndale's translation, showing how much we are indebted to him for the familiar language of the versions so well known to us:

The same daye at nyght, which was the morowe after the saboth daye, when the dores were shut, where the disciples were assembled to geder for feare of the Jewes, came Jesus and stode in the myddes, and sayd to them: peace be with you. And when he had so sayde, he showed vnto them his hondes, and his syde. Then were the disciples glad when they sawe the Lord. Then sayde Jesus to them agayne: peace be with you.

As my father sent me, even so send I you. And when he had sayde that, he brethed on them and sayde vnto them: Receave the holy goost. Whosevers synnes ye remyt they are remytted vnto them. And whosevers sins ye retayne they are retayned (John 20$^{19-23}$).

Prayer

O God, our Everliving Refuge! With grateful hearts we lay at Thy feet the folded hours when Thou knowest us but we know not Thee; and with joy receive from Thy hand once more our open task and conscious communion with Thy life and thought. Day by day liken us more to the spirits of the departed wise and good; and fit us in our generation to carry on their work below till we are ready for more perfect union with them above. And if ever we faint under any appointed cross and say, 'It is too hard to bear,' may we look to the steps of the Man of Sorrows toiling on to Calvary, and pass freely into Thy hand, and become one with Him and Thee. Dedicate us to the joyful service of Thy will; and own us as Thy children in time and in eternity. Amen.[2]

Meditation

WHAT IS THAT IN THINE HAND?

. . . Nothing in my hands I bring
Simply to Thy Cross I cling.

. . . Not what these hands have done
Can save this guilty soul;
Not what this toiling flesh has borne
Can make my spirit whole.

[2] A Prayer of James Martineau from *Great Souls at Prayer*.

   . . . O wounded hands of Jesus, build
      In us Thy new creation.

   . . . Thy hands created me, Thy hands
      From sin have set me free.

   . . . Take my hands, and let them move
      At the impulse of Thy love.

A hymn of Charles Wesley's (*M.H.B.*, No. 575)
combines the thoughts of the work of our hands, the self-
giving of Jesus on the Cross and in toil for us, and the
sacrifice of true service :

      Servant of all, to toil for man
        Thou didst not, Lord, refuse ;
      Thy majesty did not disdain
        To be employed for us.

      Son of the carpenter, receive
        This humble work of mine ;
      Worth to my meanest labour give,
        By joining it to Thine.

      End of my every action Thou,
        In all things Thee I see ;
      Accept my hallowed labour now,
        I do it unto Thee.

      Thy bright example I pursue,
        To Thee in all things rise ;
      And all I think, or speak, or do
        Is one great sacrifice.

      Careless through outward cares I go,
        From all distraction free ;
      My hands are but engaged below,
        My heart is still with Thee.

SERVICE

We have been looking at the Cross, and in one incident which happened there we may find light on the true meaning of service. At Calvary there were not only the soldiers gambling for the seamless robe,

But there were standing by the cross of Jesus his mother, and his mother's sister, Mary the wife of Clopas, and Mary Magdalene. When Jesus therefore saw his mother, and the disciple standing by, whom he loved, he saith unto his mother, Woman, behold, thy son! Then saith he to the disciple, Behold, thy mother! And from that hour the disciple took her unto his own home (John 19$^{25-7}$).

What are we to make of that incident? It may be that Jesus looked down and saw what was going on in the minds of John and Mary, and we may be sure that it was something like this: Mary, a mother watching the execution of her innocent son might well be thinking: ' After it is all over, have I to go back to the ordinary work of the home as though this had never happened? Must I go back to washing pots and cleaning rooms and cooking food after *this*?' John, the beloved disciple, watching the shameful end of his master's work must have thought: ' Have I to go back to selling fish again after seeing *this*?' And, Jesus, understanding their hearts, said: ' Woman, behold, thy son.' That housework, that drudgery of ovens and beds and waterpots, is not something you do for your own glory or comfort, but others depend upon you for it, and in return you may look to them for strength and comfort and protection. ' Behold, thy mother!' Son, that toil to which you go is not just a job, something to be done as soon as possible and then forgotten ; it is service which you can do to the glory of God, and others depend upon it for their life and well-being.

In Africa there is a tree known as the Flame of the Forest. At one season of the year its great branches are hidden in a glorious blaze of scarlet flowers. Each crimson bloom grows on the slenderest of twigs out on the tip of each tiny branch. So it is with the service offered by the Church. The massed effect of missionary work and social service ; the work of hospitals and schools ; the redemptive work of evangelism and all the healing and renewal that is brought to broken, unprivileged men are impressive when they are considered together. But when you begin to examine the picture closely you find that the flower does not grow on the trunk and the huge branches ; the service of the Church is not offered by great Assemblies—Edinburgh, Tambaram, and Amsterdam—it is personal service, offered by ordinary people like you and me. So we, the thinnest twigs in the great tree have the supreme part to play, the part of serving God and man personally as no organization can do. And it is not for nothing that early in the Covenant Service comes the parable of the vine and the branches : we cannot offer this service in our own strength.

I am the true vine, and my Father is the husbandman. Every branch in me that beareth not fruit, he taketh it away: and every branch that beareth fruit, he cleanseth it, that it may bear more fruit. Already ye are clean because of the word which I have spoken unto you. Abide in me, and I in you. As the branch cannot bear fruit of itself, except it abide in the vine ; so neither can ye, except ye abide in me. I am the vine, ye are the branches: He that abideth in me, and I in Him, the same beareth much fruit: for apart from me ye can do nothing. If a man abide not in me, he is cast forth as a branch, and is withered; and they gather them, and cast them into the fire, and they are burned. If ye abide in me, and my words abide in you, ask whatsoever ye will, and it shall be done unto you. Herein is my Father glorified, that ye bear much fruit; and so shall ye be my disciples (John 15[1-8]).

' He that abideth in Me, and I in him, the same beareth much fruit.' C. P. Groves in his book, *The Planting of Christianity in Africa*, examines the problem of North Africa, the land of the vanished Church. That country was once the home of Christian Fathers like Tertullian and Cyprian and Augustine. There the Church died because the only people it had won were swept away by Muslims, in the Arab advance from Egypt. Why? Certainly it must be admitted that the population had been greatly reduced by the Vandal wars, and that the number of Christians had been still further decreased by the bitter Ayran persecution of the Catholics. But the chief reason why the Church died out in North Africa and gave place to Islam is that it was not an evangelistic Church; it had no missionary enterprise. The great majority of the people were Berbers, the people of the countryside and villages; but they were only a tiny part of the African Church. The Church centred itself on the towns, and though Christian monasteries were established, they were very different from the monasteries of Ireland which sent out their monks to evangelize the country people. Groves sums up this unhappy account by saying: ' There is no more vivid warning that to fail to share the faith with all around is to let it die.' We are reminded of the wheat which died in the shelter of the Egyptian tomb while the wheat that sacrificed itself in the world outside went on living and increasing.

In Eastern Nigeria there is a small tribe known as the Ogoni. They are about a hundred miles from the nearest hospital, but they are visited by a missionary doctor. When he arrives with the nurse great crowds assemble for treatment who have not developed our degenerate habit of queuing—they get down to it and push. The Church is the clinic. The doctor sits in one vestry with his instruments and notebook, the nurse works in another room dispensing his prescriptions. During one visit, when the scene outside was a reminder of the story in the first chapter of Mark—' all the city was gathered together at the door '—there was suddenly a deafening noise like that of a bomb. When the dust had cleared, the doctor could see that the crowd had pushed so hard that they had pushed down part of the wall of the church. It is not that the African people have no manners, but that they knew that only a fraction of the crowd would receive attention, for later in the day a note came through from the nurse, and the doctor went to the door and said : ' Sorry friends. The medicines are finished. See you again in six months time.' You may ask what is the value of going twice a year to a place like that, and the doctor would tell you that there is much useful medical work to be done. For instance, by a few injections it is possible to cure the ghastly disease of yaws, and there are other ailments for which he can leave the medicines so that the people can treat themselves. But even more important is the psychological effect of knowing that they are not forgotten ; of being able to depend on the doctor to come on a certain day, and of being sure that he is concerned about their welfare.

The day after the collapse of the vestry wall the local chiefs called on the doctor and said that during the previous year they had been taxing their people. They had gathered nearly two thousand pounds, and they wanted the hospital to build a small clinic and instal a doctor ; they would be responsible for his salary. The doctor had no hesitation in saying that no doctor could be sent. At that time the Missionary Society had not one man in any of its medical posts in India, and there were clamorous needs in other parts of Africa and in other countries. It took a long time for those men to believe that he meant what he said and they went away depressed and puzzled. The next day they were back again, this time not with a financial proposition but with a theological problem. They said : ' For years you have been telling us that God loves us. If He loves us, why doesn't He speak to someone and tell them to come and help us ? ' I don't know how you would answer that question. I think the doctor gave the only possible reply when he said : ' I believe that God does speak to people and tell them to come and help the folk of Africa. He speaks to many people, but not everyone listens.'

If our service is in answer to the call of God, and not merely something that we think we would like to do ; if it takes us out of the shelter of our group or family or church and makes us evangelists to those who do not know Him ; if we are true branches of the vine and bear fruit because we abide in Him and He abides in us, and if we say of whatever is in our hand, whether it be camera or pen or the tool by which we earn our living, ' It is tihne, Lord. Let me use it to Thy glory and in the

5

service of others,' then we shall understand why Jesus said, ' The Son of Man came not to be served but to serve and to give his life a ransom for many.' And we shall know that truth of His great affirmation :

IT IS MORE BLESSED TO GIVE THAN TO RECEIVE

A hymn of Walter Russell Bowie (*M.H.B.*, No. 906) takes us back to our first thought, our share in the crucifying of Jesus, and reminds us that all our service is doomed if He be excluded from it :

> Lord Christ, when first Thou cam'st to men,
>   Upon a Cross they bound Thee ;
> And mocked Thy saving Kingship then
>   By thorns with which they crowned Thee :
> And still our wrongs may weave Thee now
> New thorns to pierce that steady brow,
>   And robe of sorrow round Thee.
>
> O awful love which found no room
>   In life where sin denied Thee,
> And, doomed to death, must bring to doom
>   The power which crucified Thee,
> Till not a stone was left on stone,
> And all a nation's pride o'erthrown
>   Went down to dust beside Thee.
>
> New advent of the love of Christ,
>   Shall we again refuse Thee,
> Till in the night of hate and war
>   We perish as we lose Thee ?
> From old unfaith our souls release
> To seek the Kingdom of Thy peace,
>   By which alone we choose Thee.

O wounded hands of Jesus, build
  In us Thy new creation ;
Our pride is dust, our vaunt is stilled,
  We wait Thy revelation :
O love that triumphs over loss,
We bring our hearts before Thy Cross,
  To finish Thy salvation.

THE COVENANT

Here, the people standing, the Minister shall say,

And now, beloved, let us bind ourselves with willing
bonds to our covenant God, and take the yoke of
Christ upon us.

This taking of His yoke upon us means that we are
heartily content that He appoint us our place and
work, and that He alone be our reward.

Christ has many services to be done ; some are easy,
others are difficult ; some bring honour, others bring
reproach ; some are suitable to our natural inclinations
and temporal interests, others are contrary to both.
In some we may please Christ and please ourselves, in
others we cannot please Christ except by denying
ourselves. Yet the power to do all these things is
assuredly given us in Christ, who strengtheneth us.

Therefore let us make the Covenant of God our own.
Let us engage our heart to the Lord, and resolve in His
strength never to go back.

Being thus prepared, let us now, in sincere dependence
on His grace and trusting in His promises, yield
ourselves anew to Him, meekly kneeling upon our
knees.

5*

Here shall the Minister say in the name of all :

O Lord God, Holy Father, who hast called us through Christ to be partakers in this gracious Covenant, we take upon ourselves with joy the yoke of obedience, and engage ourselves, for love of Thee, to seek and do Thy perfect will. We are no longer our own, but Thine.

Here all the People shall join :

I am no longer my own, but Thine. Put me to what Thou wilt, rank me with whom Thou wilt ; put me to doing, put me to suffering ; let me be employed for Thee or laid aside for Thee, exalted for Thee or brought low for Thee ; let me be full, let me be empty ; let me have all things, let me have nothing ; I freely and heartily yield all things to Thy pleasure and disposal.

And now, O glorious and blessed God, Father, Son and Holy Spirit, Thou art mine, and I am Thine. So be it. And the Covenant which I have made on earth, let it be ratified in heaven. Amen.

PART TWO

The Cross

Suggestions for Bible Study and Questions for Discussion

These Notes are divided into four sections : (a) The Cross Caused by Sin ; (b) The Cross as Victory ; (c) The Cross and Me ; (d) The Cross Proclaimed.

(A) THE CROSS CAUSED BY SIN

1. WHAT IS SIN ?

The group might discuss this question before looking at the following references.

(a) *Putting self first.*

Self-will : rebellion against God, Hosea 10^{12-13}, Amos 2^4, Romans 5^{10}, 8^7, James 4^4. (Contrast Psalm 40^{6-8}, quoted Hebrews 10^{5-9}. See also Philippians 2^{19-30}. N.B. verses 21 and 30.)

Self-worship : putting self in place of God, Genesis 3^5, Psalms 36^{1-2}, quoted Romans 3^{18}. See also Romans 1^{21}.

Selfishness : self-centredness, Mark 8^{35} ; thinking of self before others, Amos 4^{1-2}, 5^{11-12}, 8^{4-6}, Matthew 18^{23-35}. (Contrast Luke 10^{25-37}, 19^{8-9}.)

(b) *Blindness.*

Isaiah 6^{9-10} : it seems clear that Jesus must have quoted this passage from Isaiah on more than one occasion : see Matthew 13^{14}, Mark 4^{11}, Luke 8^{10}, John 12^{40}. Also Acts 28^{26}. (Contrast Isaiah 29^{18}, 35^5.)

2 Corinthians 4^{3-6}: compare 2 Corinthians 3^{7-18} (especially verse 14), 1 Corinthians 1^{18}, 2^{14}. Also Matthew 15^{14}, 2 Peter 1^9, Revelation 3^{17}.

Wilful choice of darkness: John 3^{19}.

(c) Falling short of the glory of God.

Romans 3^{23}: read 2 Corinthians 3, remembering that in the Bible the meaning of the word *glory* alternates between the sense of the splendour of the visible appearance of God and the manifestation of the nature and purpose of God, which can only be understood spiritually.

God is glorified not merely in revealing His goodness to men, but in attracting them to Himself so that His goodness is reproduced in them and they are made in His image (2 Corinthians 3^{18}).

Missing the mark: this is the root meaning of the Greek word for sin, Hosea 6^{4-6}, Luke 10^{38-42}, 11^{39}, 12^{15-34}, John 12^{43}.

Losing the Way: Isaiah 53^6, Romans 3^{12}. Compare St. Augustine's saying: 'Thou hast made us for Thyself and our hearts can find no rest till they find rest in Thee.' Hymn 467.

Worshipping false gods: Hosea 11^{1-2}, Luke 16^{13}.

(d) Death.

Colossians 2^{13}, Ephesians $2^{1,5}$. Compare the following:

Ephesians $2^{1,5}$: dead in sins;
quickened with Christ.

Romans 8^{10-11}: the body dead because of sin;
the spirit life because of righteousness.

Galatians 2^{20} :   I am crucified with Christ ;
                        Yet Christ lives in me.

Now read Romans 6 in which the two ideas are brought together :

Sin brings death (Romans 6$^{21, 23}$).

The Christian is dead to sin (Romans 6^6).

Luke 9^{60}, 1 Corinthians 1^{18} (note the phrase 'they that are perishing' ; again in 2 Corinthians 2^{15}, 2 Thessalonians 2^{10}).

See Hymn 756.

In all this, note :

(i) Man's sense of helplessness in his sin (Romans 7$^{18, 19, 24}$).

(ii) The assertion of Jesus that sin is alien to God's world (Matthew 13$^{24-30}$).   (Note again the idea of enmity, and compare Genesis 3^{15}, 2 Corinthians 4^4, Ephesians 2^2).

2.   HOW DID SIN CRUCIFY JESUS ?

(a) *Through those who were living at the time.*

What part had the following in the matter ?

Caiaphas : Matthew 26$^{3-4}$, John 11$^{47-53}$, Mark 14$^{53-65}$. Study this character in Dorothy Sayers' *The Man Born to be King*.

Pilate : John 18^{28}—19^{16}, especially 19$^{8-12}$, Acts 4^{27}.

Judas : Mark 3$^{14, 19}$, Luke 22$^{3-6}$, Mark 14$^{18-21}$, Luke 22$^{47-9}$.

What about Peter ? Luke 22$^{54-62}$. (Read also Mark 1$^{16-18}$, Matthew 16$^{13-18}$, John 13^{36}—14^1, Mark 14$^{37-8, 66-72}$, Mark 16^7.)

(b) What about ourselves ?

Romans 3^{23}, Philippians 3^{18-19}.

Am I prone to put my own interests first ?

Am I prone to find good reasons for doing wrong actions ?   (John 11^{47-53}.)

3. PLATO, FOUR HUNDRED YEARS BEFORE CHRIST, PROPHESIED THAT IF EVER A PERFECT MAN CAME UPON THIS EARTH MEN WOULD CRUCIFY HIM

Why do you think he made this prophecy ?

Read the following passages and decide what more must be said about the death of Jesus than is contained in the statement of Plato :

(a) The frequent prophecies of Jesus about His own death : e.g. Mark 8^{31}, 9^{31}, 10^{33-4}.

(b) Such passages as : Luke 22^{22}, Acts 2^{23}, 3^{18}, 4^{28}, Romans 8^{32}, Ephesians 1^{3-12} (N.B. verses 4 and 7), 1 Peter 1^{19-20}, Revelation 13^{8}.

See Hymn 175, verse 1.

(B) THE CROSS AS VICTORY

Did Jesus really win ? (John 16^{33}).   What sort of victory was it ?

1. THE VICTORY OF GOOD FRIDAY

(a) The victory of unbeaten love.

John 13^1 : having loved His own, those in the world, *to the utmost* (not 'to the end'), showed He His love to them.

John 10^{11}, 15^{13}.

Luke 23^{43}: even His love for those who put Him to death was not vanquished. See Hymn 187, verse 7.

(b) *The victory of the Cross over*:

Man's enmity against God: Romans 5^{10}, 2 Corinthians 5$^{14-18}$, Ephesians 2^{16}, Colossians 1$^{19-22}$.

Sin: Romans 5^{19}, 6$^{1-10}$, 2 Corinthians 5^{21}, Galatians 1^{4}, 6^{14}, Ephesians 1^{7}, Hebrews 10$^{1-10}$, 1 Peter 1$^{18-19}$.

The power of the flesh: Romans 6^{6}, Galatians 2^{20}, 5^{24}, Colossians 3$^{1-3}$.

The curse of the law: Galatians 3^{13}, 4^{5}, Colossians 2^{14}.

(c) *The victory of the undeflected purpose*.

John 16^{33}: He did not conform to this world's standards and methods. Romans 12$^{1-2}$, Ephesians 2$^{15-16}$ and 4$^{23-4}$, 1 Peter 1$^{13-19}$, 1 John 2$^{15-17}$.

The world could not make Him change His direction: Matthew 5^{8}; 'pure in heart' means more than 'clean'; it means having the will set straight toward God in simplicity of purpose. Compare the idea of 'renew a right spirit within me' in Psalms 51^{10}; and see also James 1^{8}.

Mark 10$^{32-4}$, Luke 9^{51}, John 11$^{8, 16}$.

(d) *Jesus spoke of His death as being glorified*.

   (i) When the Greeks came to Him (John 12$^{23-8}$).

   (ii) When Judas had gone out into the night (John 13$^{31-2}$).

(iii) When the time came for Him to be 'lifted up' (John 12$^{32, 34}$).

John 17^1.

Read also Hebrews 12$^{1-2}$.

2. THE VICTORY OF EASTER DAY

The victory of Good Friday would have been incomplete without the victories of Easter and Pentecost (Romans 8^{34}).

(a) *Victory over death.*

Romans 6^9, 1 Corinthians 15$^{54-7}$, Hebrews 2$^{14-15}$.

Hymn 756.

(b) *Victory over the powers of darkness.*

John 1^5: 'The light shineth in the darkness and the darkness did not *absorb it*.' A.V., comprehended; R.V., apprehended; R.V., margin, overcame.

The word has two meanings. Its root sense is 'to take cover, or, under'; thus it comes to mean either: to take right into the mind (apprehend), or to take under control (overcome). The darkness was neither able to understand nor to dim the light. In both senses of the word the passage is true.

(c) *Victory in the disciples.*

What about Peter now? John 21^{15ff}, Acts 2^{14ff}, 4^{13ff}.

3. THE VICTORY OF PENTECOST

Love available in power today through the Holy Spirit, Romans 5^5.

Love the supreme gift of the Holy Spirit, 1 Corinthians 13.

The victory that overcometh the world, 1 John 5^{4-5}.

Was Jesus really victorious? John 16^{33}, 1 John 5^{4-5}. (These are the quotations with which this section began and ended.)

(c) THE CROSS AND ME

What does the Cross mean for me? Read Hymn 371.

1. IN WHAT WAY DID I CAUSE HIS PAIN?

(Hymn 371, verse 1.)

(*a*) Where should we have stood at the time of the Crucifixion? Acts 4^{27}.

(*b*) We share in the common guilt of mankind, Isaiah $53^{5-6, 10}$, Rom. 3^{23}, 4^{25}, 2 Corinthians 5^{21}, 1 Peter 3^{18}.

(*c*) We can crucify Him afresh today, Hebrews 6^6. (Hymn 906, verse 1.)

2. IN WHAT WAY DID CHRIST DIE FOR ME?

(Verse 1.)

Galatians 2^{20}. See also Romans 6^6, 14^{7-9}, 2 Corinthians 5^{14-15}, Galatians 1^4, 6^{14}, 1 Thessalonians 5^{10}, Titus 2^{14}, 1 Peter 2^{24}, 3^{18}, 4^2.

3. WHAT IS MEANT BY SAYING THAT IT IS ALL MERCY?

(Hymn 371, verse 3.)

Ephesians 2^5, $^{8-9}$.

'So free, so infinite His grace.' Even the faith by which we are saved is a gift of God, or it would still be by our own work that we are saved.

See also Romans 3¹⁹⁻²⁵, 4¹⁶, Titus 3⁴⁻⁷. The word translated 'propitiation' in Romans 3²⁵ would be better rendered by some such word as 'cleansing.' A modern equivalent would be 'decontamination.' A related word is used in Luke 18¹³ ('Lord *be merciful* to me a sinner').

4. HAS IT FOUND OUT ME?

(Hymn 371, verse 3.)

Compare Galatians 1⁴ with Galatians 2²⁰.

5. WHAT DOES IT MEAN TO FOLLOW HIM?

(Hymn 371, verse 4.)

(a) Mark 8³⁴⁻⁵, Colossians 1²⁴.

(b) *Share His experiences.*

Baptism: 1 Corinthians 12¹³.

Persecution: John 15¹⁹⁻²⁰.

Transfiguration: Romans 12², 2 Corinthians 3¹⁸. 'Transformed' and 'changed' in these two passages are used to translate the same word as that rendered 'transfigured' in Matthew 17². See also Philippians 3²¹.

Crucifixion: Romans 6⁶⁻⁸, Galatians 2²⁰, Philippians 3¹⁰. (Hymn 598, verse 4.)

Death: Romans 6⁵, 1 Corinthians 15³¹, Colossians 2²⁰, 3³, 2 Timothy 2¹¹.

Burial: Romans 6⁴, Colossians 2¹².

Resurrection: John 14¹⁹, Romans 6⁵, ⁸⁻⁹, 8¹¹, Galatians 2²⁰, Ephesians 2¹, ⁵, Philippians 3¹⁰, Colossians 2¹², 3¹, 2 Timothy 2¹¹.

Ascension : The Collect for Ascension Day reads : 'Grant, we beseech Thee, Almighty God, that like as we do believe Thy only-begotten Son our Lord Jesus Christ to have ascended into the heavens ; *so we may also in heart and mind thither ascend*, and with Him continually dwell, who liveth and reigneth with Thee and the Holy Ghost, one God, world without end. Amen.'

Appearance : Colossians 3^4.

Read Hymn 204, verse 4.

(*c*) *Become like Him.*

Irenaeus (about A.D. 112) answering the question, 'Why did God become man ?' said, 'Out of His infinite love He became what we are that we might become what He is.' 2 Corinthians 5^{21}, 8^9, Philippians 2^7, 3^{21}. Hymn 372.

Romans 8^{29}, Ephesians 4^{13}, 2 Peter 1^4, 1 John 3^2.

Read Hymn 465, verse 5.

6. IS THE BOLDNESS OF VERSE 5 JUSTIFIED ?

(Hymn 371, verse 5.)

(*a*) Ephesians 3^{11-12}, Hebrews 4^{14-16}, 10^{16-22}, 1 John 2^{28}, 3^{21}, 4^{17}, 5^{14}.

(*b*) It is a question of what God is like rather than whether or not we are worthy to become before His presence. Matthew 11^{28-30}, Luke 15^2, $19^{7, 10}$, John 3^{17}, Luke 5^{32}, 1 Timothy 1^{15}.

SUMMARY OF SECTIONS A, B AND C

In Section A we saw that sin may be regarded as :

putting self at the centre of life in place of God ;

blindness to truth and goodness as revealed by God ;
falling short of the glory of God ;
being dead because of separation from God.

How does this link with Section B (the victory of the
Cross) and C (the Cross and me) ?

Self: Galatians 2^{20}. Has the love of Christ been
victorious in me, making Him the centre of my life ?
Is *this* what is meant by, 'It found out me' ? (Hymn
371, verse 3.)

Blindness: John 9^{25}. Has the love of Christ been
victorious in me so that in His light I see light ?
(Hymn 371, verse 4.)

Glory: 2 Corinthians 3^{18}. Has the love of Christ been
victorious in transforming me into His likeness ? Is
this what is meant by 'Jesus and all in Him is mine' ?
(Hymn 371, verse 5.)

Death: Romans 6^{11}. Has the love of Christ been
victorious in me so that I am dead to sin but alive to
God ? 'Alive in Him my living Head.' (Hymn 371,
verse 5.)

(D) The Cross Proclaimed

How shall we tell men what has been done for them ?

1. BY WHAT WE ARE

Rom. 12^1, 14^{13}, 2 Corinthians 4^{1-2}, 6^{1-4a}, Philippians
1^{12-14}, 2^{14-16}.

Read the whole of 2 Corinthians 5 and 6.

2. WHY DID JESUS CHOOSE TWELVE DISCIPLES ?

Mark 3^{14} : sent forth to *preach*.

Note the importance of preaching. See also 1 Corinthians 1^{21-4}, Colossians 1^{28}. (In 1 Corinthians 1^{21} the reference is to the foolishness of *the* preaching, that is, the facts preached, e.g. the Resurrection of Jesus.)

John 15^{11-17}.

Compare John 8^{12} and Matthew 5^{14}. See also John 1^9, 20^{21}.

3. THE CELL OR GROUP AS THE UNIT OF LIFE

Acts $2^{41-2, 46}$.

(a) Find out all you can about the early Methodist Class Meetings, e.g. from *John Wesley and the Methodist Societies*, by J. S. Simon.

(b) Find out all you can about the constitution and function of communist cells, e.g. from *Soviet Communism*, by Sidney and Beatrice Webb, pp. 355ff.

(c) Find out all you can about the cell as the unit of life in plants and animals ; the way in which growth occurs by the division of cells ; the doctrine of cells, e.g. from *Biology for Everyman*, by J. A. Thomson, pp. 972 and 1027. (There is an interesting quotation from St. Paul in the second reference.)

(d) Read the following on the place of the congregation in evangelism : *The World Mission of the Church*, *Tambaram*, 1938, p. 31 (The essential task of the Church). *Toward the Conversion of England*, pp. 130-2. *We shall rebuild*, by Geo. McLeod, pp. 91-8.

4. WHAT ARE THE MARKS OF A CHRISTIAN CELL ?

In addition to these marks of the Christian cell which you have already discussed, note that such a cell should be :

(a) *Organized for evangelism.* Mark 3^{14}, 6^7.

The following definition of evangelism was given by the Archbishop's Commission on Evangelism in 1918, it was accepted by the World Meeting of the International Missionary Council at Tambaram in 1938, and quoted in *Toward the Conversion of England* (1945) : 'To evangelize is so to present Christ Jesus in the power of the Holy Spirit, that men shall come to put their trust in God through Him, to accept Him as their Saviour, and serve Him as their King in the fellowship of His Church.'

The cell should also be ready to work *inside* the cell by discussion and study ; *outside* the cell by witness and by service.

(b) *A community of unlikes in which all are equal.* Galatians 3^{28}.

Brought together by a common loyalty to Christ, John 1^{12}, 17$^{11, 21}$, 1 Corinthians 1$^{9-13}$, Galatians 3^{26}, 1 John 1^3, 2^{24}. In which men find God, 1 Corinthians 14^{25}.

(c) *Prepared to accept the sacrifice of division.*

As we saw under D3(c), all living things grow by the division of cells, one becomes two, two become four, and so on. A Christian cell should have between six and twelve members. It should aim at splitting into two new cells as soon as possible. This principle is frequently forgotten.

The problem of splitting is the problem of finding new leaders.

The group should be looking for likely leaders, and should see that they are being trained.

Is your cell between six and twelve in number?

Is it growing?

What is the cell doing about training new leaders?

5. WHAT DO WE MEAN BY SAYING THAT THE CHURCH
   IS THE BODY OF CHRIST?

(a) Romans 12$^{3-5}$, 1 Corinthians 11$^{27-9}$, 12$^{12-27}$, Ephesians 1$^{22-3}$, 3^{6}, 4$^{11-13}$, Colossians 1^{24}.

(b) The Church is the instrument through which the Holy Spirit continues the work of Christ on earth. We are part of the body, so we are part of the Gospel. ('I believe in the Holy Catholic Church.') This means enmity with the world. (Compare A1(a) in which sin was seen to be enmity with God.) We are members of each other. The obvious thing about a body is that it cannot be divided into separate parts. *What about our divisions and denominations in view of this description of the Church as the Body of Christ?* 1 Corinthians 1^{13}.

'We have a foretaste of the reality of the Body of Christ and the blessed company of all faithful people when we experience:

'That sense of fellowship and oneness with fellow-believers from all races, cultures and nationalities, which triumphs even over the tension created by the bitterness created by war and conflict;

'that sense of Christian community that arises from sharing with fellow-believers in the organized life of the Church through its worship, its sacraments, its witness and its works; and 'that sense of being soldiers of the Cross which unites us with our fellow-believers in the great fight under Christ's banner against all the forces of paganism and irreligion in the world around us.'[1]

6. WHY DO WE FEEL IMPELLED TO PROCLAIM THE CROSS TO THE WHOLE WORLD ?

(a) Because we are commanded to do so, Matthew 28[18-20].

Thus it is not a matter of choice but of necessity, John 12[49], Acts 13[4], 1 Corinthians 9[16].

The root meaning of the word missionary is 'one who is sent.'

As Jesus was sent by the Father, so He sends us, Mark 3[14], John 17[18], 20[21].

He sends us first into the work that lies nearest at hand, then farther afield, then to the ends of the earth, Acts 1[8].

(b) The Christian Gospel is for the whole world, not for some special part of it :

The vocation of Israel was to be the missionary of God to the nations, Isaiah 49[6]. This is the theme of the Book of Jonah.

The New Israel has the same vocation, Luke 24[47]. All men are the brethren for whom Christ died, John 1[29], 3[16], 15[11-12], 1 Corinthians 8[11], Revelation 5[9]. (Hymn 114, verse 7.)

The Old and New Testaments look for the day when all nations shall acknowledge God, Psalm 86[9], Micah 4[1-2], Revelation 7[9], 15[4].

(c) Read the argument of Paul in Romans 10[9-15].

[1] From *The World Mission of the Church* (findings of the Tambaram Conference), p. 28.